VOL. 122

HAL•LEONARD®
GUITAR
PLAY-ALONG

AUDIO
ACCESS
INCLUDED

CROSBY, STILLS & NASH

PLAYBACK+
Speed • Pitch • Balance • Loop

To access audio visit:
www.halleonard.com/mylibrary

Enter Code
3334-3005-3632-6636

Cover photo © Amalie R. Rothschild

ISBN 978-1-4234-9205-4

HAL•LEONARD®
7777 W. BLUEMOUND RD. P.O. BOX 13819 MILWAUKEE, WI 53213

Visit Hal Leonard Online at
www.halleonard.com

GUITAR NOTATION LEGEND

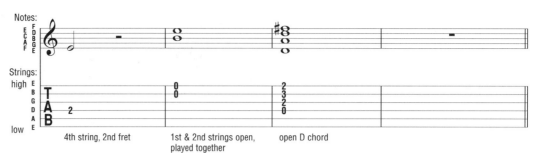

THE MUSICAL STAFF shows pitches and rhythms and is divided by bar lines into measures. Pitches are named after the first seven letters of the alphabet.

TABLATURE graphically represents the guitar fingerboard. Each horizontal line represents a string, and each number represents a fret.

4th string, 2nd fret

1st & 2nd strings open, played together

open D chord

HALF-STEP BEND: Strike the note and bend up 1/2 step.

WHOLE-STEP BEND: Strike the note and bend up one step.

GRACE NOTE BEND: Strike the note and immediately bend up as indicated.

SLIGHT (MICROTONE) BEND: Strike the note and bend up 1/4 step.

BEND AND RELEASE: Strike the note and bend up as indicated, then release back to the original note. Only the first note is struck.

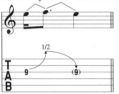

PRE-BEND: Bend the note as indicated, then strike it.

VIBRATO: The string is vibrated by rapidly bending and releasing the note with the fretting hand.

PALM MUTING: The note is partially muted by the pick hand lightly touching the string(s) just before the bridge.

HAMMER-ON: Strike the first (lower) note with one finger, then sound the higher note (on the same string) with another finger by fretting it without picking.

PULL-OFF: Place both fingers on the notes to be sounded. Strike the first note and without picking, pull the finger off to sound the second (lower) note.

LEGATO SLIDE: Strike the first note and then slide the same fret-hand finger up or down to the second note. The second note is not struck.

SHIFT SLIDE: Same as legato slide, except the second note is struck.

TRILL: Very rapidly alternate between the notes indicated by continuously hammering on and pulling off.

TAPPING: Hammer ("tap") the fret indicated with the pick-hand index or middle finger and pull off to the note fretted by the fret hand.

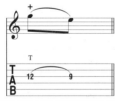

NATURAL HARMONIC: Strike the note while the fret-hand lightly touches the string directly over the fret indicated.

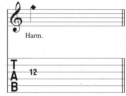

PINCH HARMONIC: The note is fretted normally and a harmonic is produced by adding the edge of the thumb or the tip of the index finger of the pick hand to the normal pick attack.

TREMOLO PICKING: The note is picked as rapidly and continuously as possible.

VIBRATO BAR DIVE AND RETURN: The pitch of the note or chord is dropped a specified number of steps (in rhythm), then returned to the original pitch.

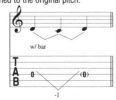

VIBRATO BAR SCOOP: Depress the bar just before striking the note, then quickly release the bar.

VIBRATO BAR DIP: Strike the note and then immediately drop a specified number of steps, then release back to the original pitch.

Additional Musical Definitions

(accent)

- Accentuate note (play it louder).

(staccato)

- Play the note short.

D.S. al Coda

- Go back to the sign (%), then play until the measure marked "***To Coda***," then skip to the section labelled "**Coda**."

D.C. al Fine

- Go back to the beginning of the song and play until the measure marked "***Fine***" (end).

Fill

N.C.

- Label used to identify a brief melodic figure which is to be inserted into the arrangement.

- Harmony is implied.

- Repeat measures between signs.

- When a repeated section has different endings, play the first ending only the first time and the second ending only the second time.

HAL•LEONARD®
GUITAR
PLAY-ALONG

AUDIO
ACCESS
INCLUDED

VOL. 122

CONTENTS

Carry Me

Words and Music by David Crosby

Drop D tuning, Capo II:
(low to high) D-A-D-G-B-E

Intro
Moderately slow ♩ = 94

*Symbols in parentheses represent chord names respective to capoed guitar.
Symbols above reflect actual sounding chords. Capoed fret is "0" in tab.

Verse

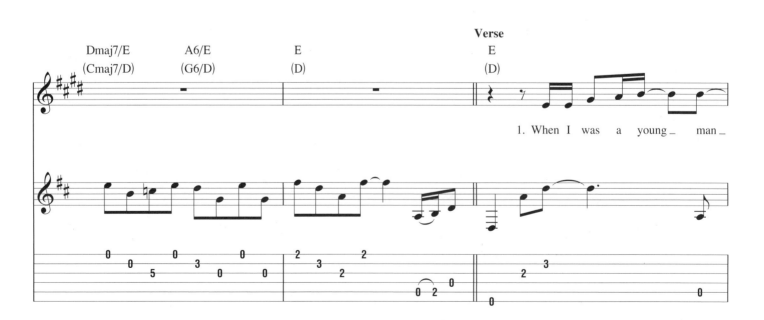

1. When I was a young_ man_

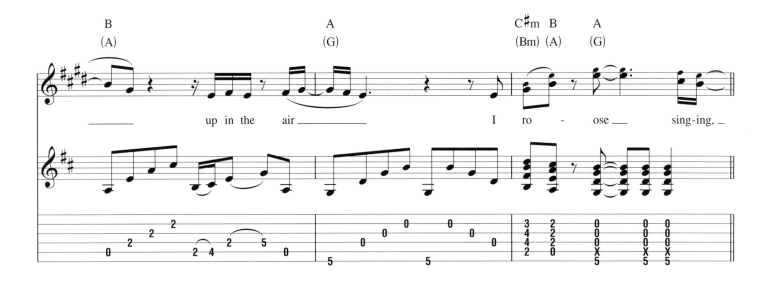

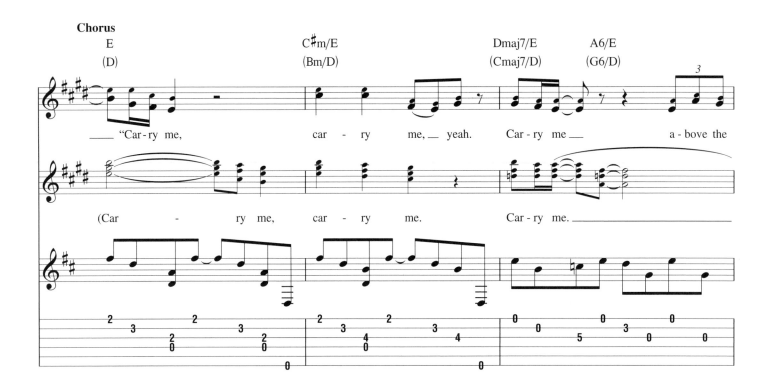

Verse

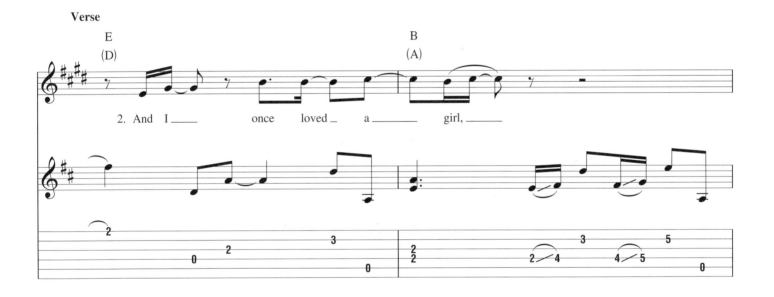

Her par-ents kept her locked up in their life, _____ and she was

cry-ing at night. She was wish-ing she could __ be _____ free. _____

Spoken: Course I most - ly re-mem - ber her laugh - ing, _____

stand - ing there and watch - ing us play. _____

Chorus

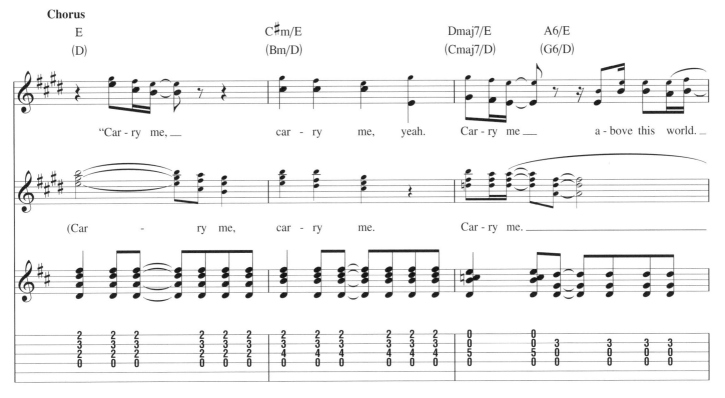

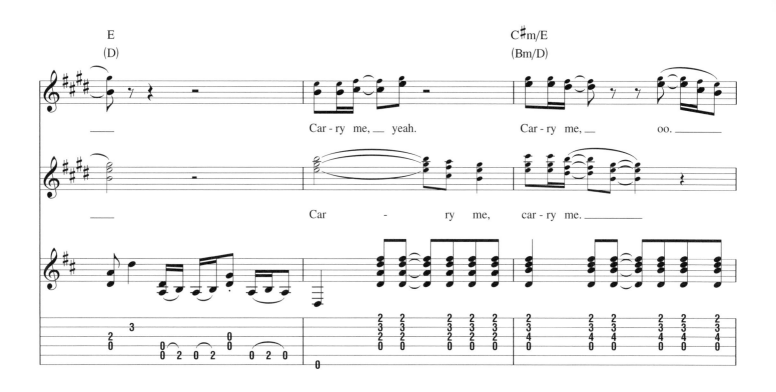

Car - ry me, __ yeah. Car - ry me, __ oo. __

Car - - ry me, car - ry me.

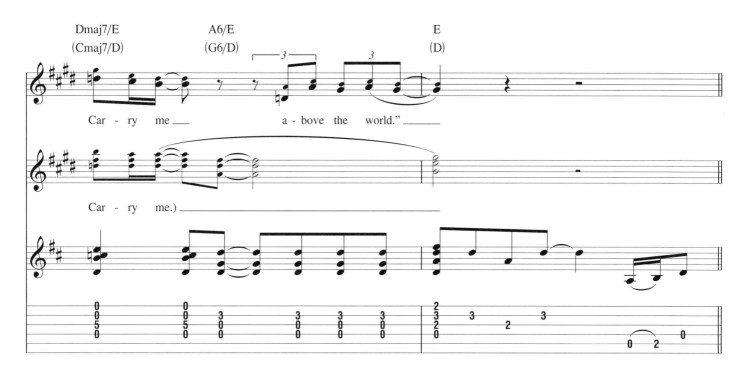

Car - ry me __ a - bove the world." __

Car - ry me.)

Verse

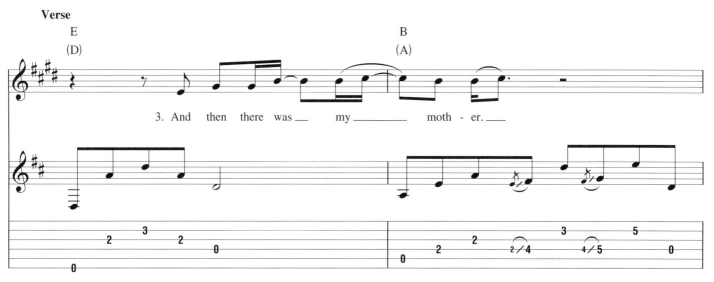

3. And then there was __ my __ moth - er. __

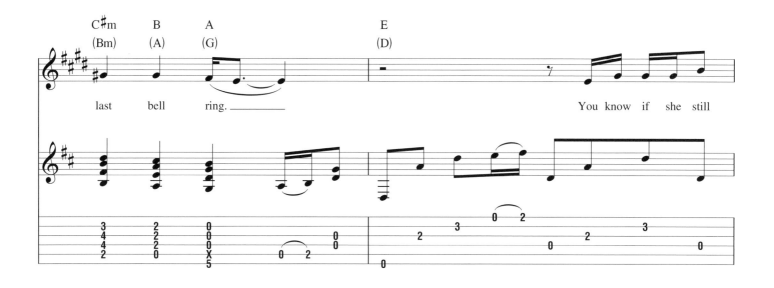

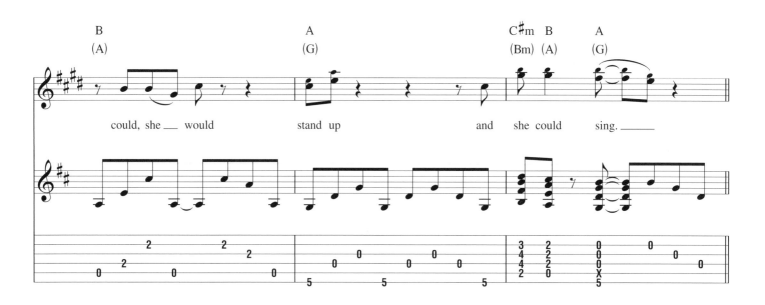

Outro-Chorus

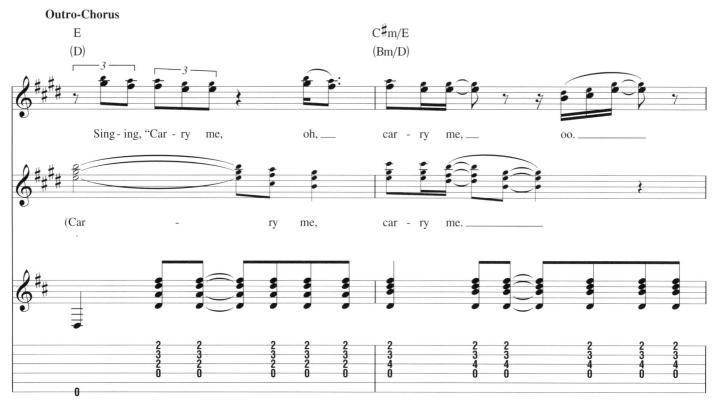

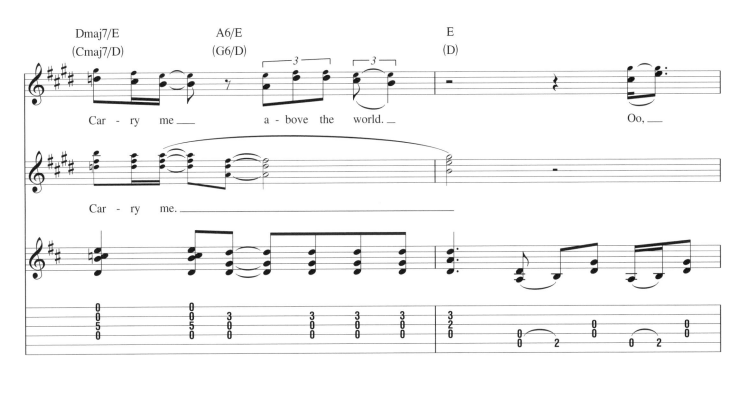

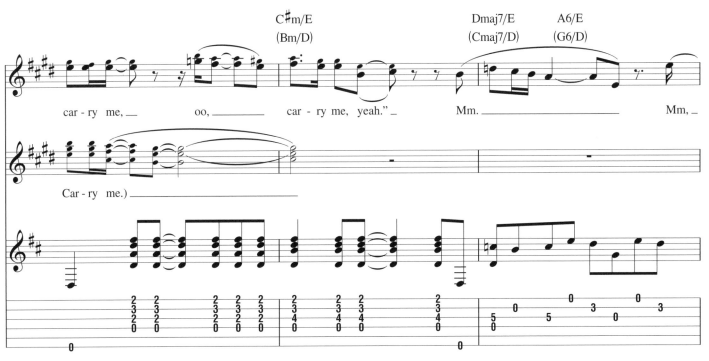

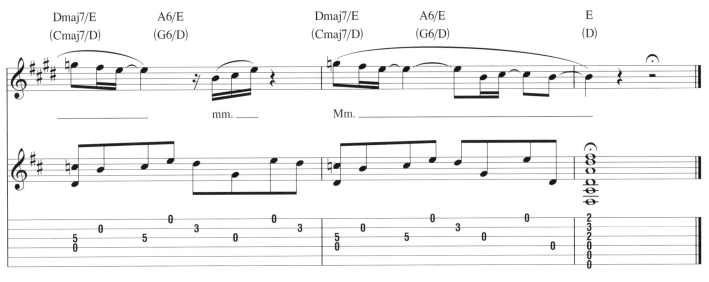

Déjà Vu

Words and Music by David Crosby

Open Em11 tuning:
(low to high) E-B-D-G-A-D

Intro
Moderately ♩ = 116

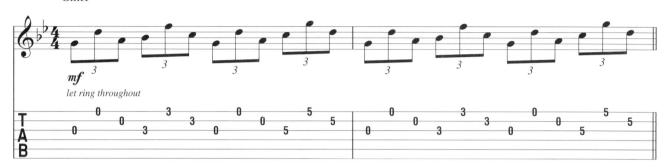

One, two, three, four.

Play 9 times

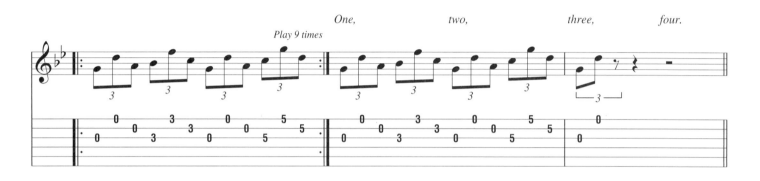

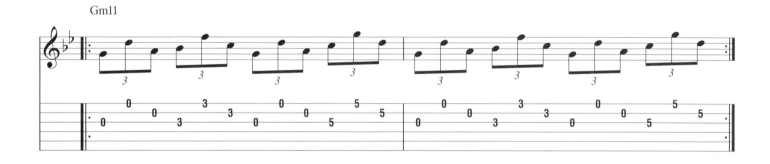

Verse

Gm11

1. If I had ev-er been here be-fore, I would prob-a-bly know just what to do.

Don't you?

If I had ev-er been here be-fore on an-oth-er time a-round the wheel, __ I would prob-'bly

know just how to deal __ with all of you.

Slower ♩ = 69

Em11

And I

Interlude

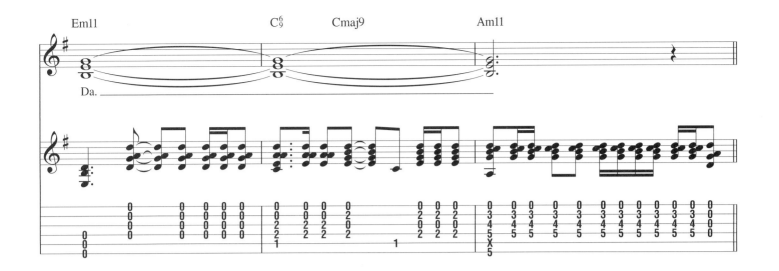

Outro

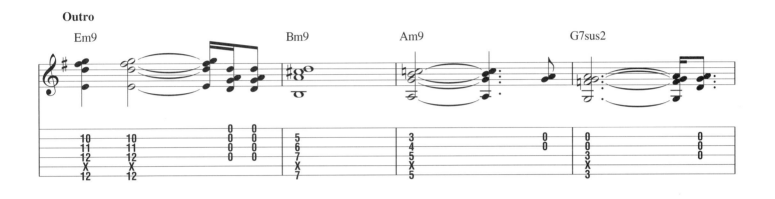

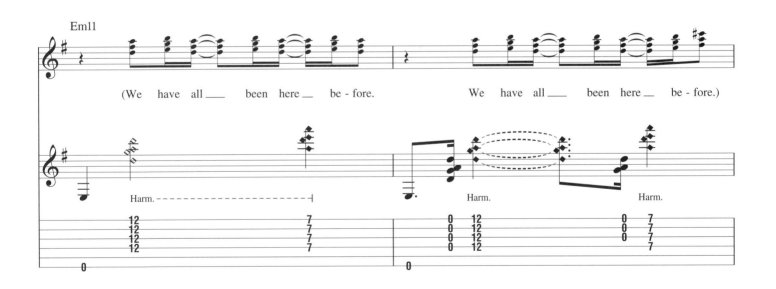

(We have all ___ been here ___ be-fore. We have all ___ been here ___ be-fore.)

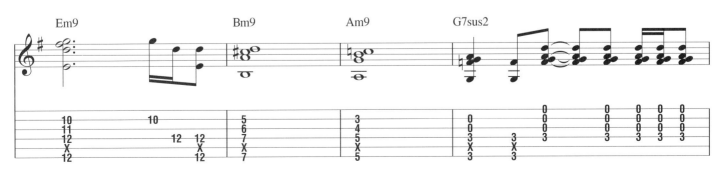

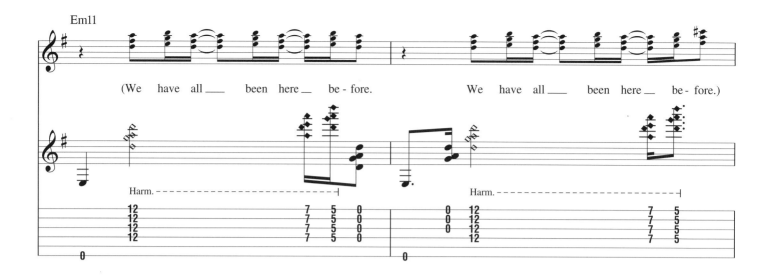

(We have all ___ been here ___ be - fore. We have all ___ been here ___ be - fore.)

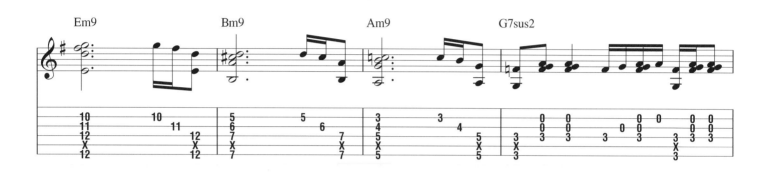

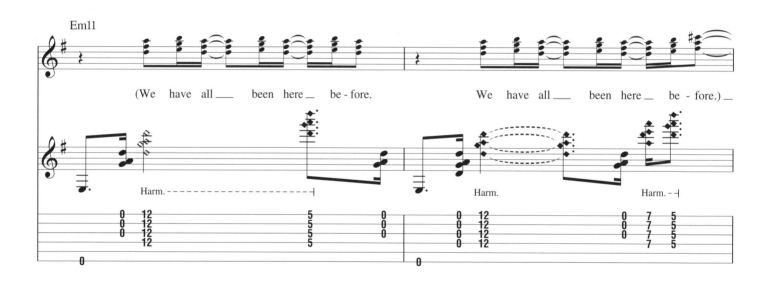

(We have all ___ been here ___ be - fore. We have all ___ been here ___ be - fore.) ___

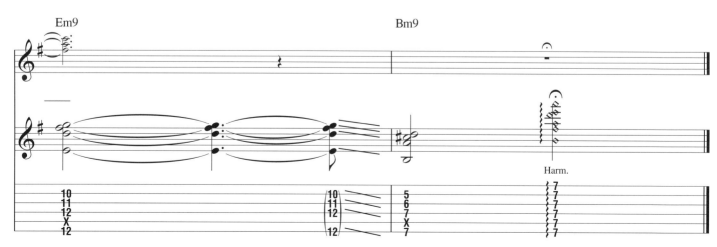

Southern Cross

Words and Music by Stephen Stills, Richard Curtis and Michael Curtis

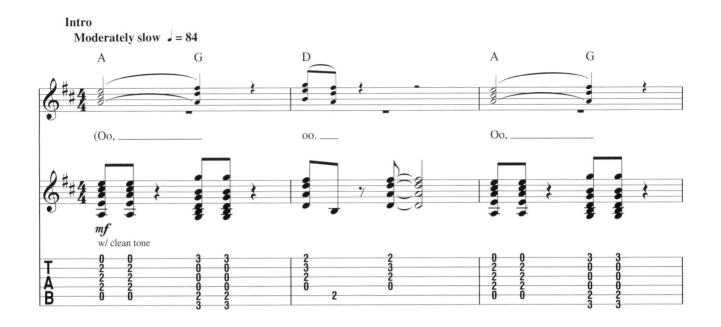

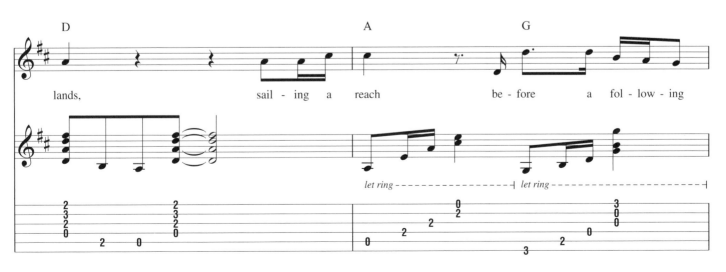

Interlude

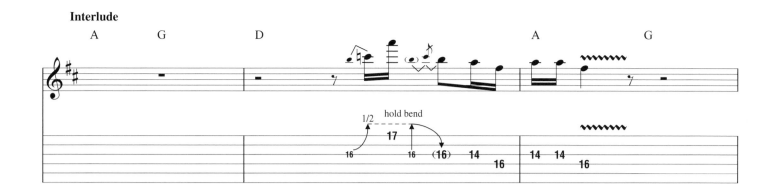

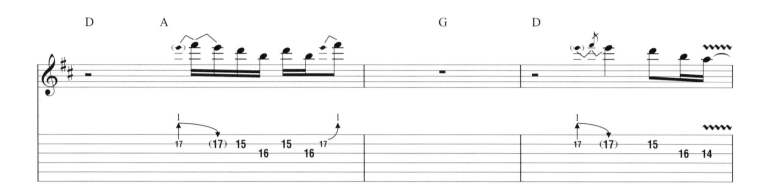

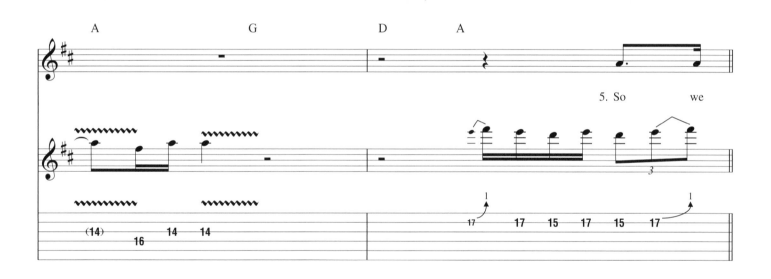

5. So   we

Verse

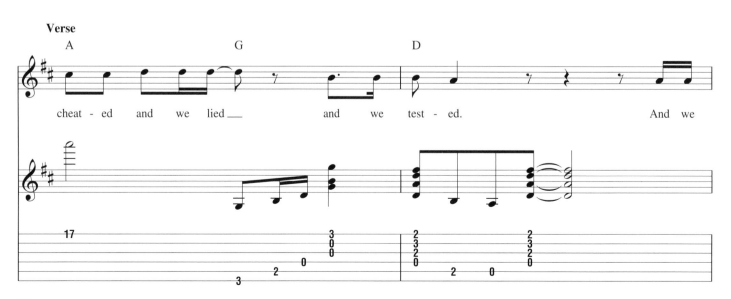

cheat - ed and we lied ___   and we test - ed.   And we

Just a Song Before I Go

Words and Music by Graham Nash

Capo II

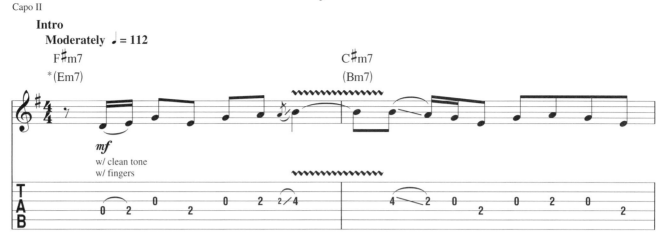

*Symbols in parentheses represent chord names respective to capoed guitar.
Symbols above reflect actual sounding chords. Capoed fret is "0" in tab.

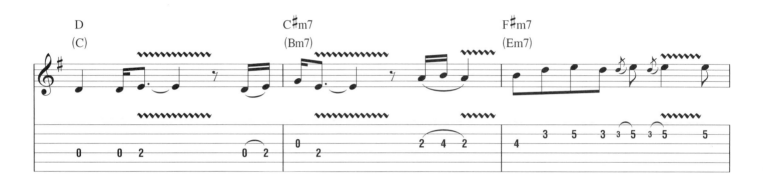

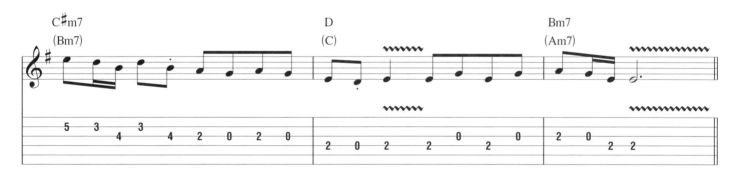

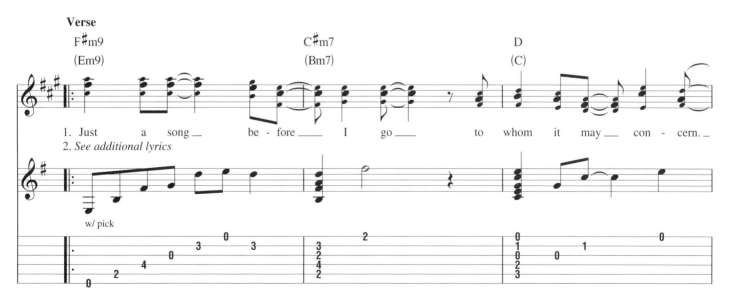

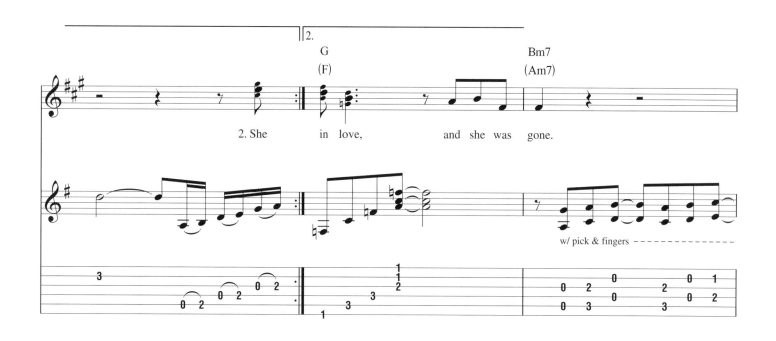

2. She __ in love, __ and she was gone.

Guitar Solo

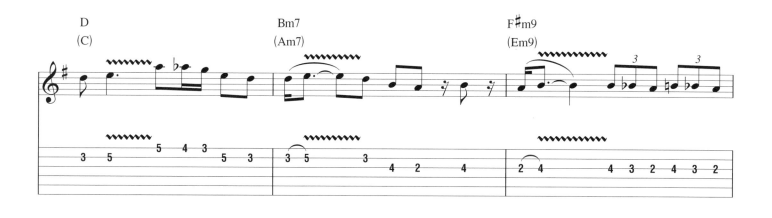

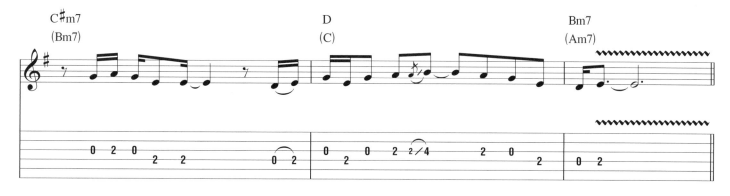

Outro-Verse

Additional Lyrics

2. She helped me with my suitcase, she stands before my eyes.
   Driving me to the airport and to the friendly skies.
   Going through security, I held her for so long.
   She fin'lly looked at me in love, and she was gone.

Marrakesh Express

Words and Music by Graham Nash

Intro
Moderately fast ♩ = 216

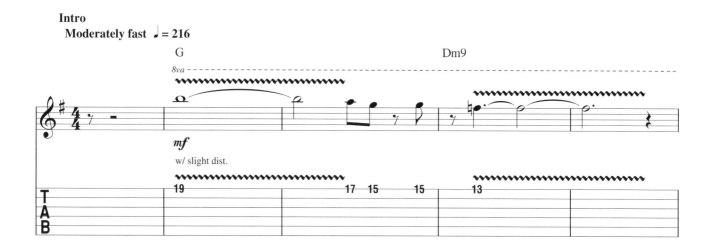

Verse

1. Look - in' at _____ the world _____ through the sun - set in _____ your eyes, _____

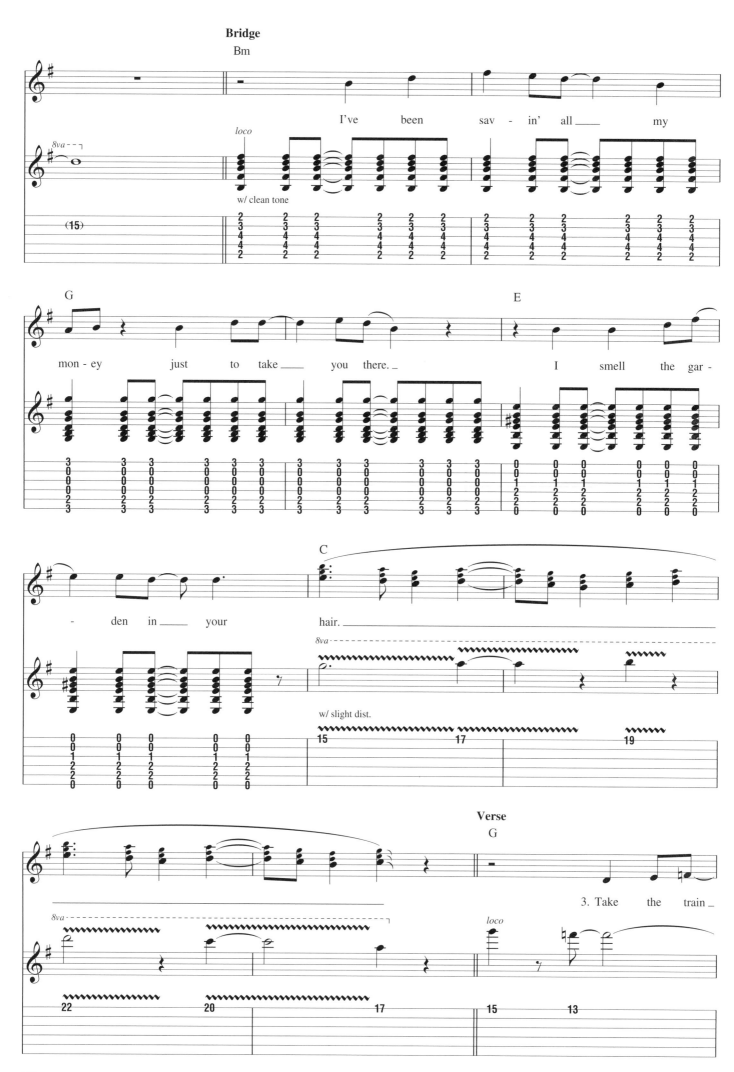

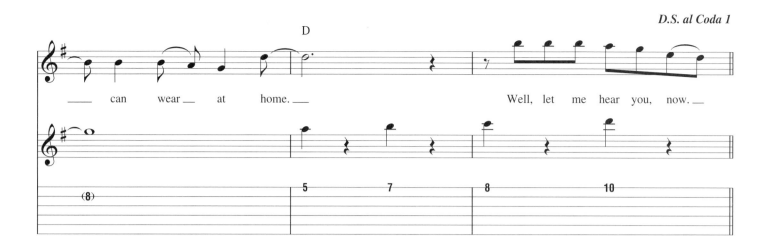

can wear at home. Well, let me hear you, now.

Coda 1

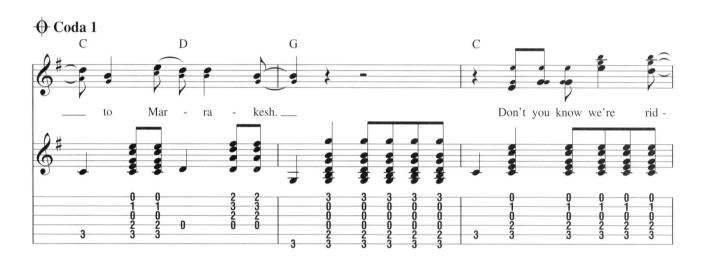

to Mar - ra - kesh. Don't you know we're rid -

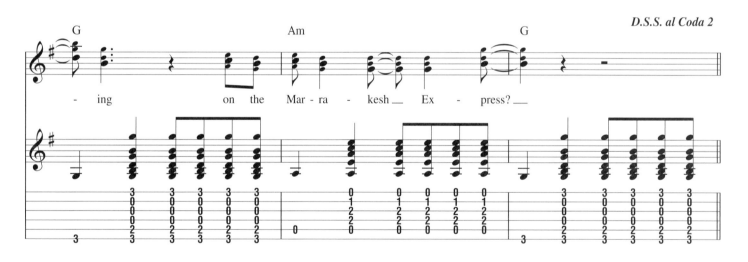

-ing on the Mar - ra - kesh Ex - press?

Coda 2

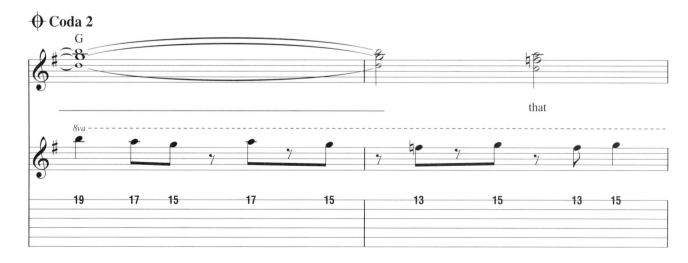

that

Suite: Judy Blue Eyes

Words and Music by Stephen Stills

Open E5 tuning:
(low to high) E-E♭-E-E-B-E

Intro

Moderately fast ♩ = 152

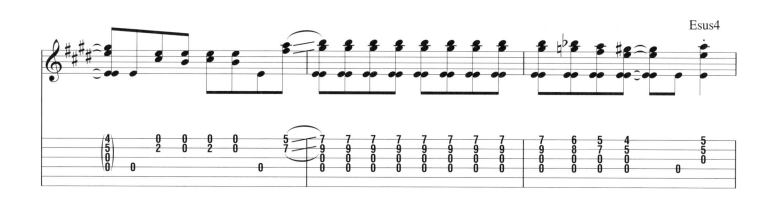

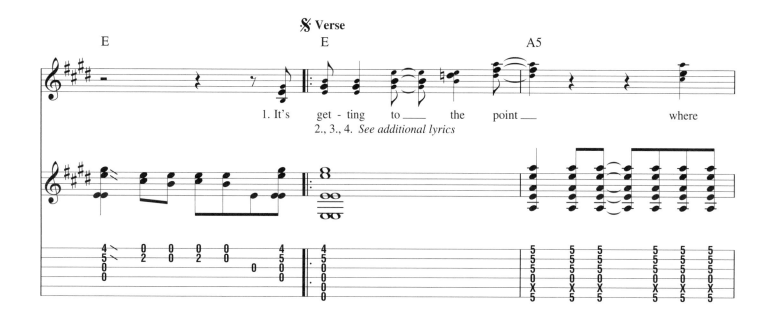

1. It's get-ting to _____ the point _____ where
2., 3., 4. *See additional lyrics*

I'm no fun an-y -more. ___

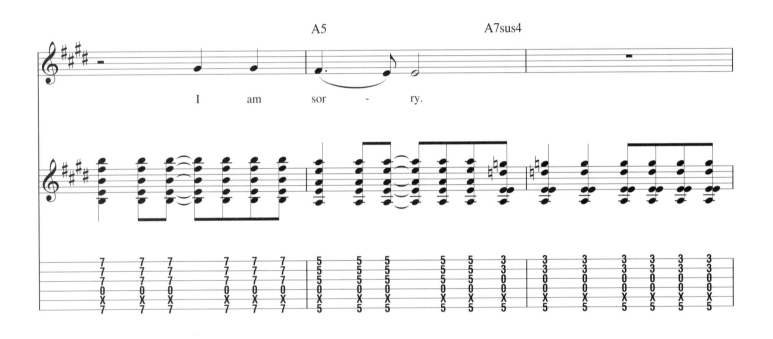

I am sor - ry.

Some - times it hurts ___ so bad - ly I must cry ___ out loud. ___

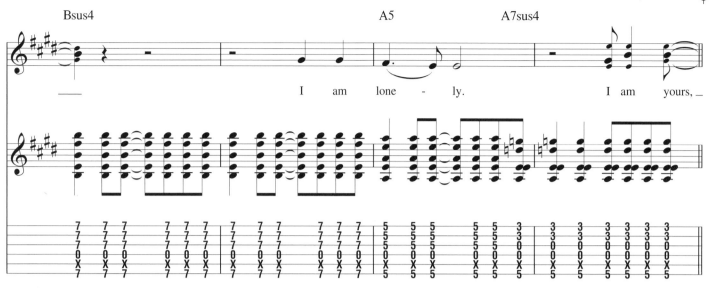

Chorus

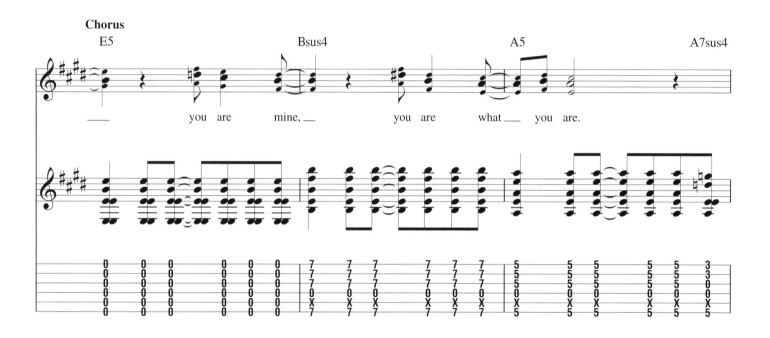

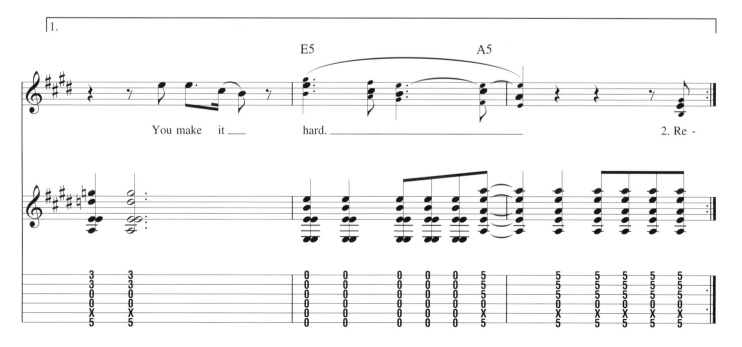

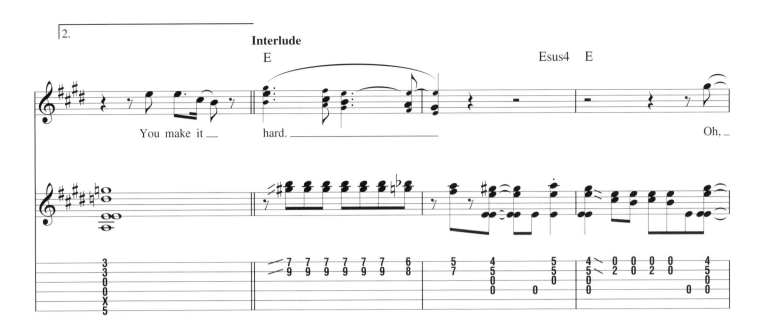

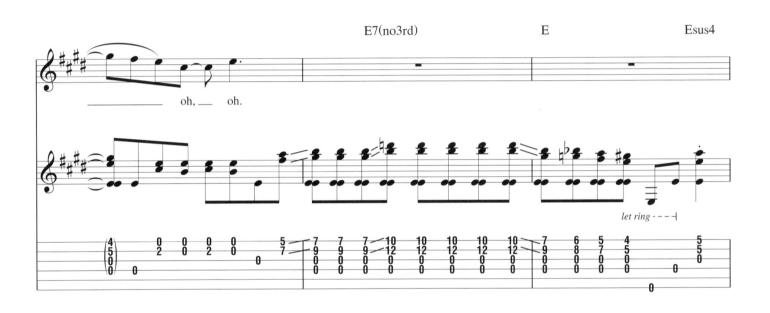

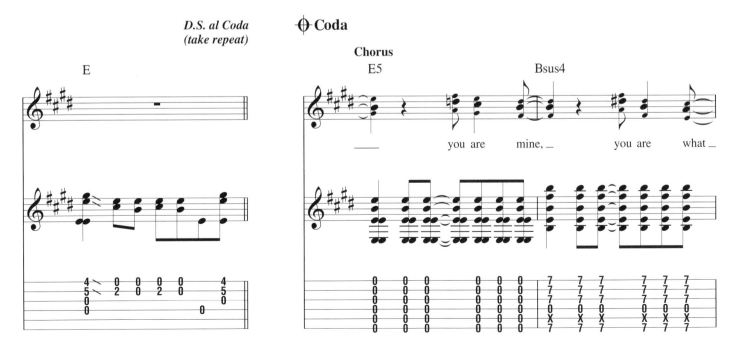

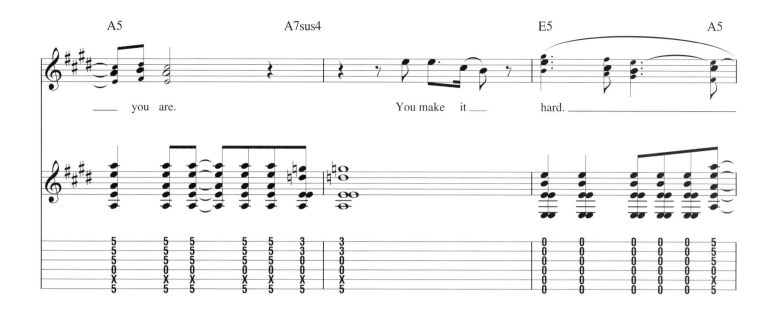

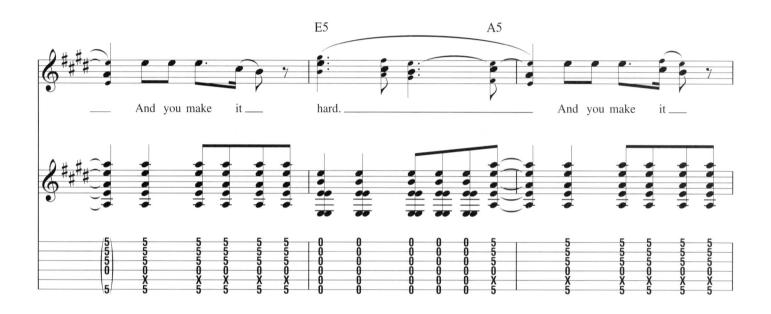

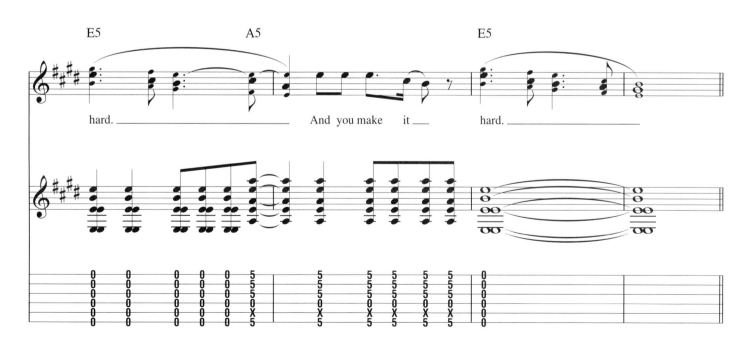

Interlude
Half-time ♩ = 76

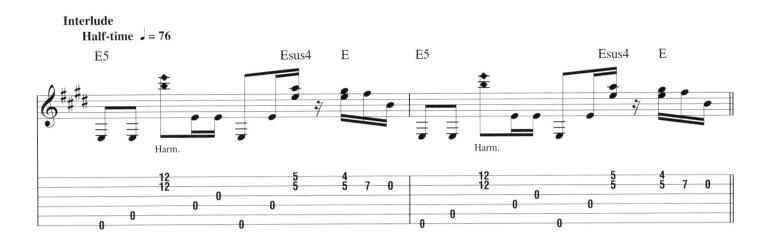

Bridge

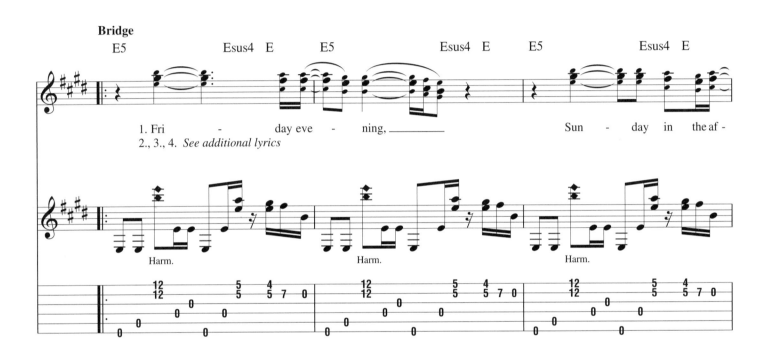

1. Fri - day eve - ning, _____ Sun - day in the af -
2., 3., 4. *See additional lyrics*

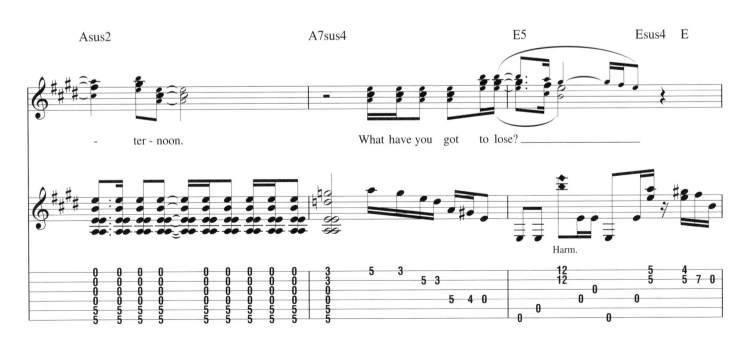

- ter - noon. What have you got to lose? _____

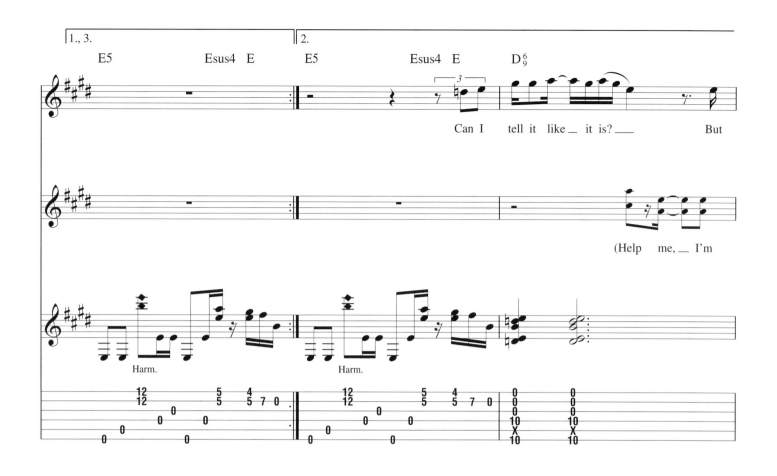

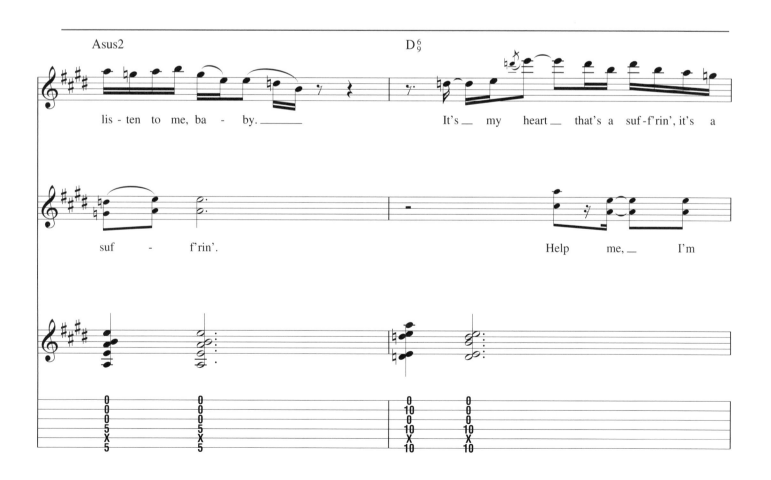

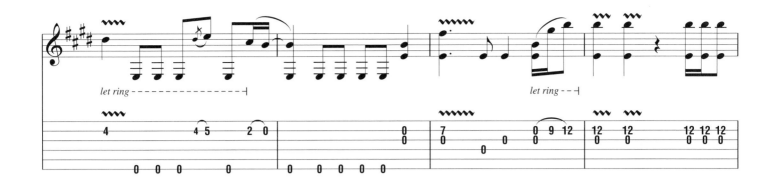

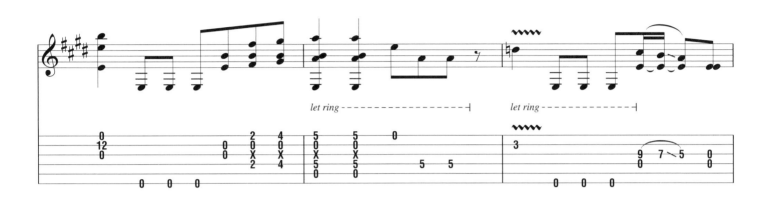

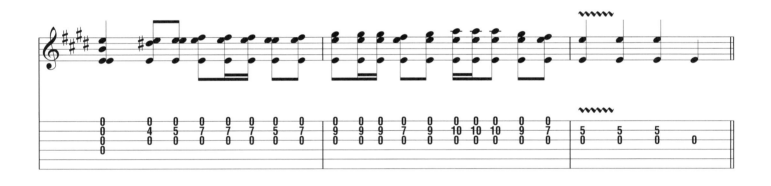

Verse

5. Chest - nut   brown __ ca - nar - - - - - y, _____   ru - by   throat - ed   spar -
   6. *See additional lyrics*

row, sing a song, ___ don't be long, ___

thrill me to ___ the mar - row. ___

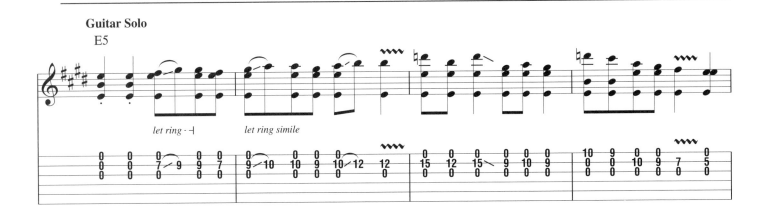

Guitar Solo

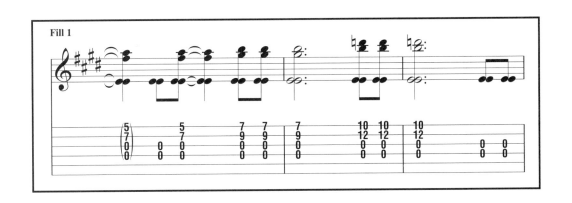

Fill 1

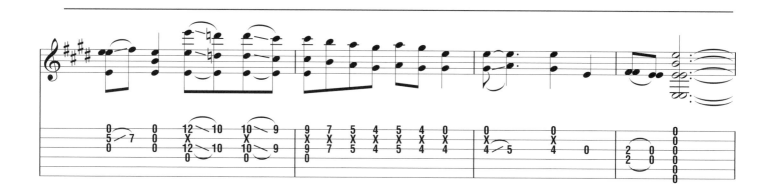

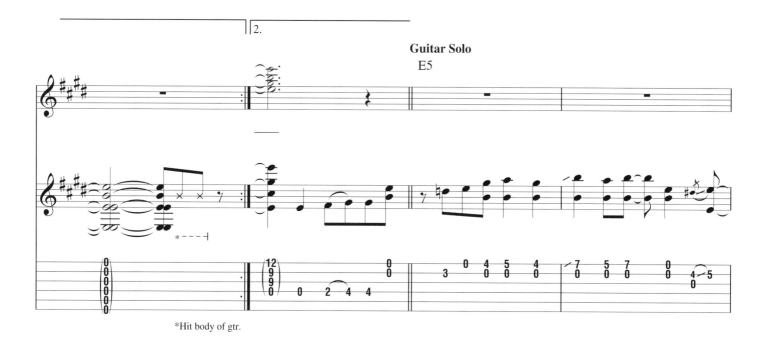

Guitar Solo

E5

*Hit body of gtr.

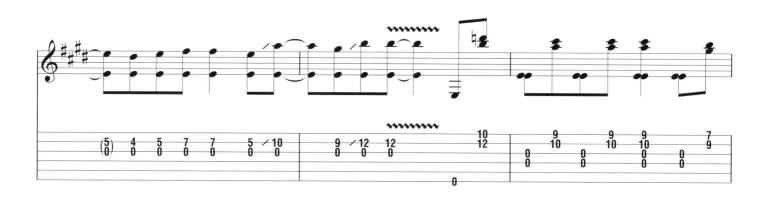

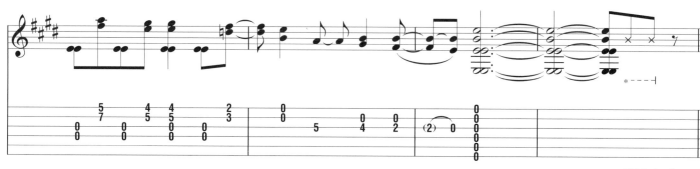

*Hit body of gtr.

Verse

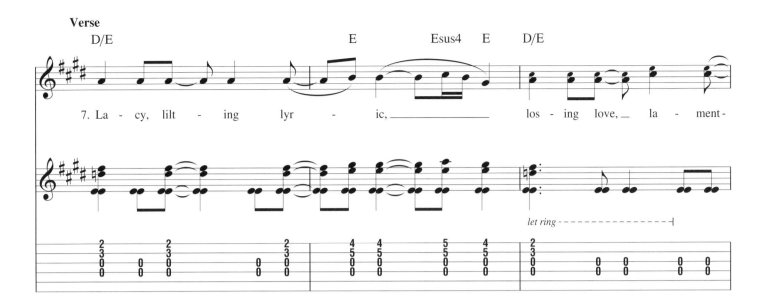

7. La - cy, lilt - ing lyr - ic, _____ los - ing love, __ la - ment-

- ing, change _ my life, _ make _ it right, _ be my la -

Interlude

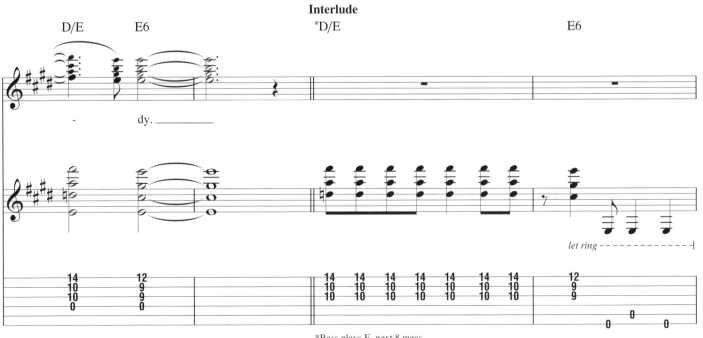

- dy. _____

*Bass plays E, next 8 meas.

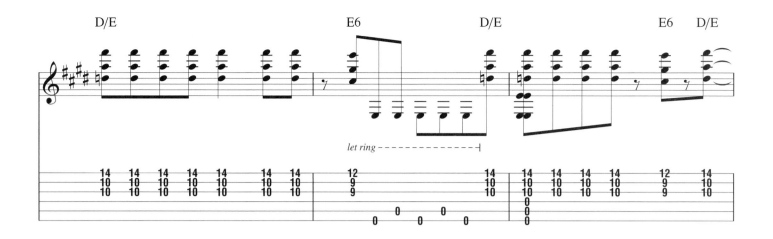

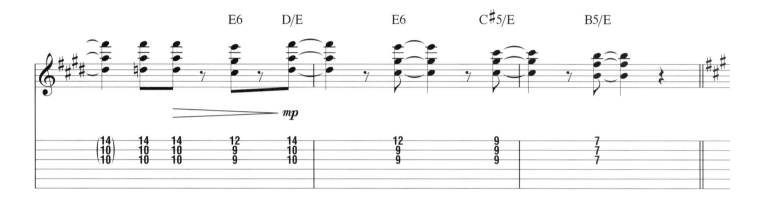

Outro
Gtr. tacet

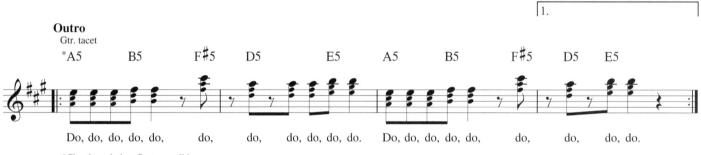

Do, do, do, do, do,   do,   do,   do, do, do.   Do, do, do, do, do,   do,   do,   do, do.

*Chord symbols reflect overall harmony.

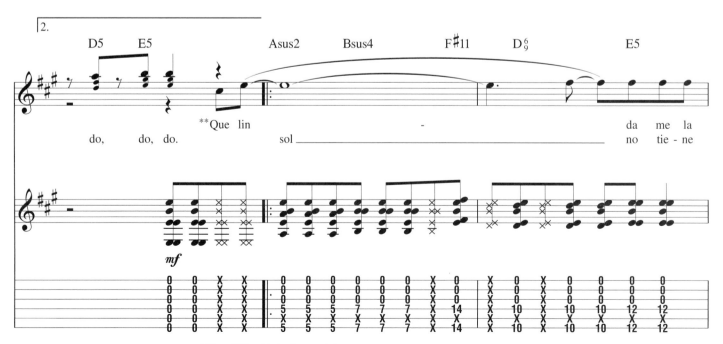

**See additional lyrics for translation.

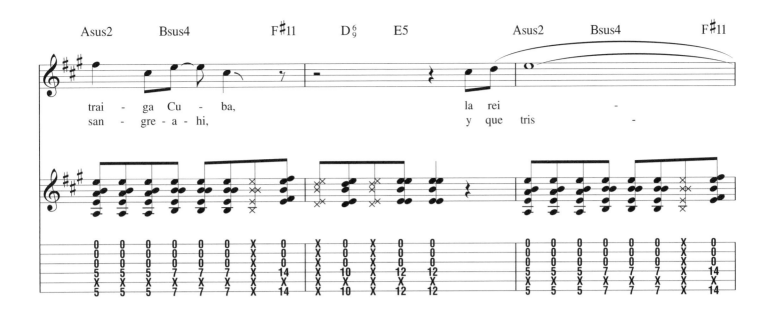

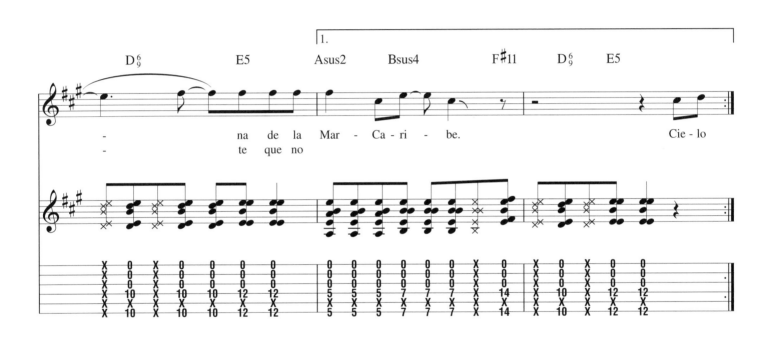

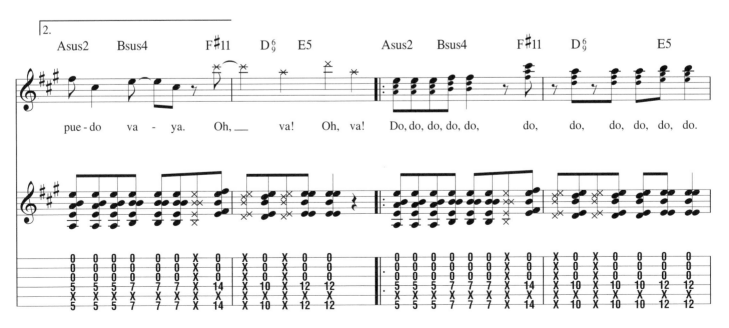

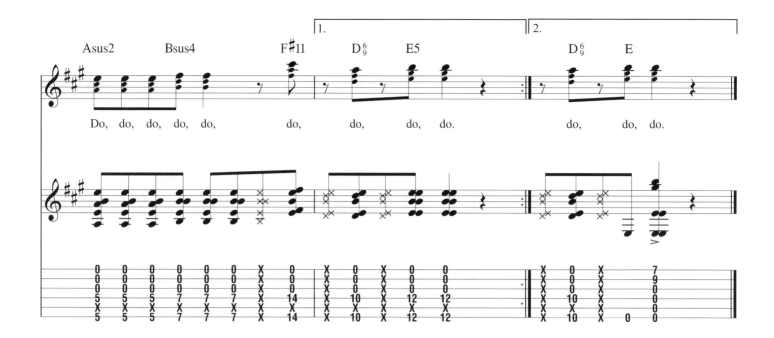

Additional Lyrics

2. Remember what we've said and
   Done and felt about each other.
   Oh, babe, have mercy.
   Don't let the past remind us of
   What we are not now.
   I am not dreaming.

3. Tearing yourself
   Away from me now,
   You are free, and I am crying.
   This does not mean I don't love you,
   I do, that's forever,
   Yes, and for always.

4. Something inside is telling me that
   I've got your secret.
   Are you still list'ning?
   Fear is the lock and
   Laughter the key to your heart.
   And I love you.

Bridge 2. Tuesday morning,
   Please be gone, I'm tired of you.
   What have you got to lose?

Bridge 3. I've got an answer,
   I'm going to fly away.
   What have I got to lose?

Bridge 4. Will you come see me
   Thursdays and Saturdays? Hey, (hey,) hey.
   What have you got to lose?

6. Voices of the angels, ring around the moonlight,
   Asking me, said she so free,
   "How can you catch the sparrow?"

Outro translation:
   How happy it makes me to think of Cuba,
   The smiles of the Caribbean Sea.
   Sunny sky has no blood,
   And how sad that I'm not able to go.
   Oh, go! Oh, go!

Teach Your Children

Words and Music by Graham Nash

Drop D tuning:
(low to high) D-A-D-G-B-E

Intro

Moderately slow ♩ = 78

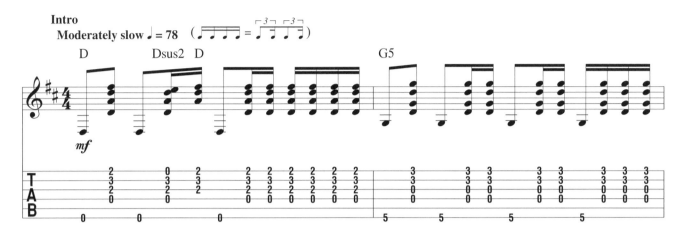

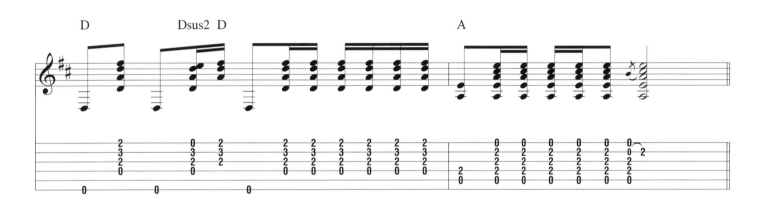

Verse

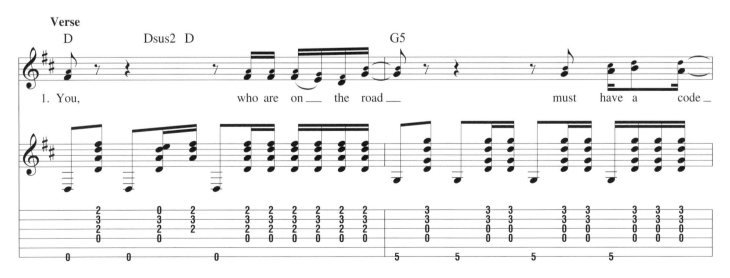

1. You, who are on __ the road __ must have a code __

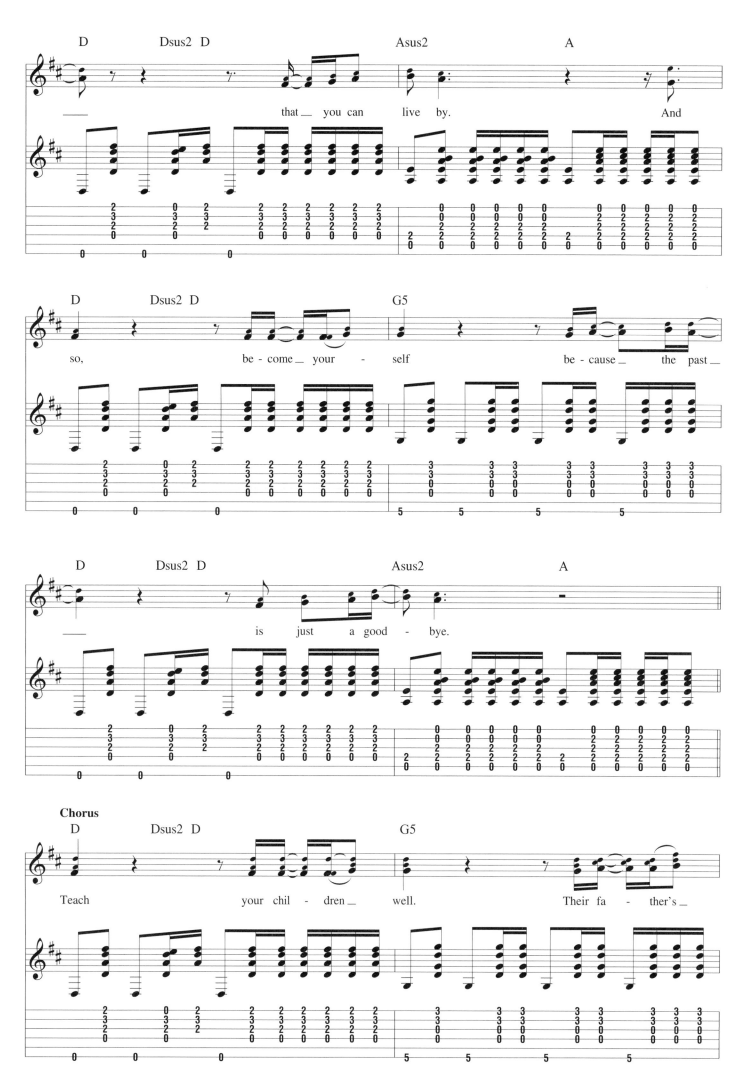

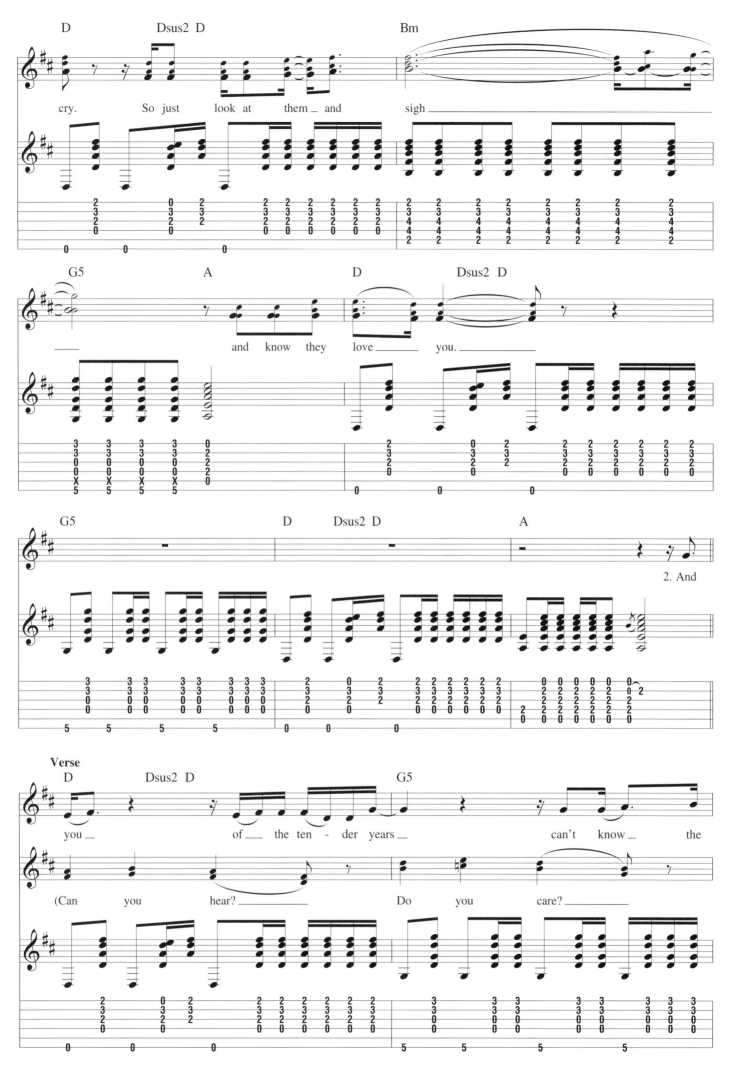

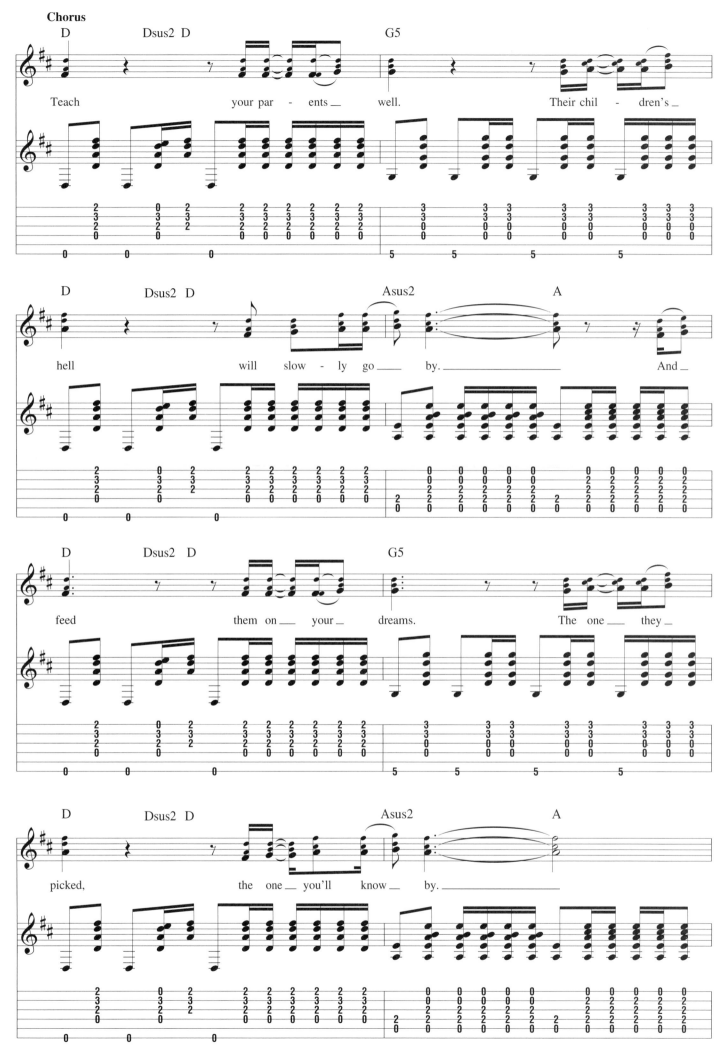

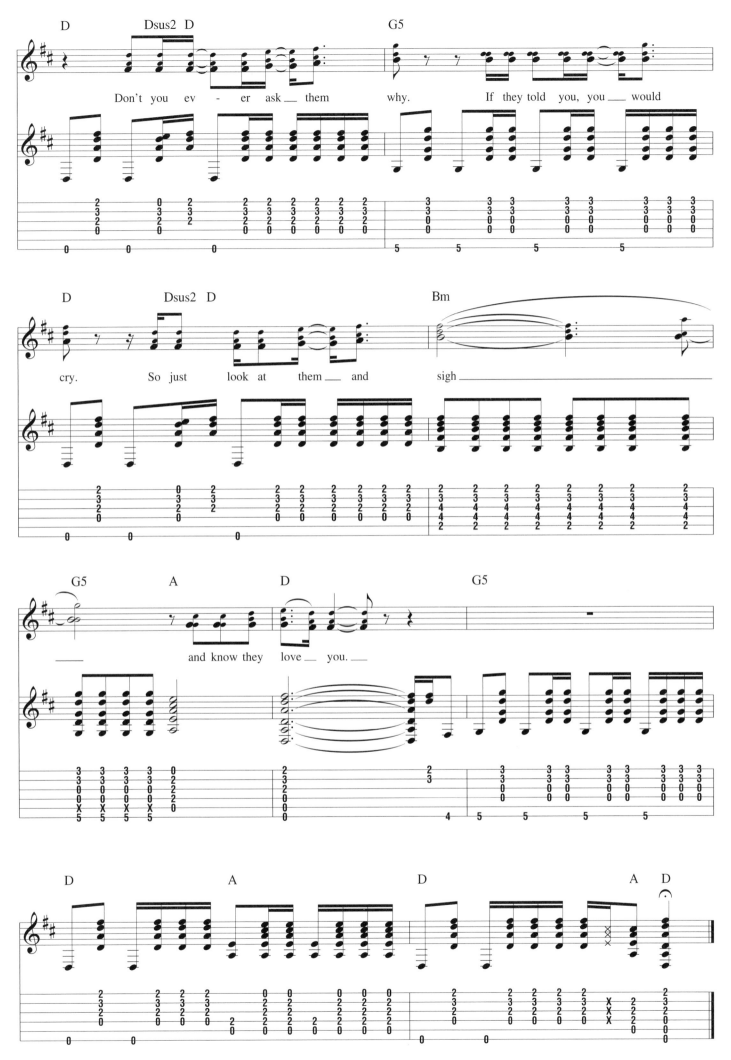

Wasted on the Way

Words and Music by Graham Nash

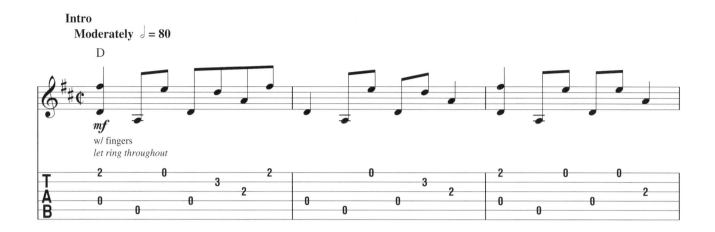

1. Look a - round _____ me, I can

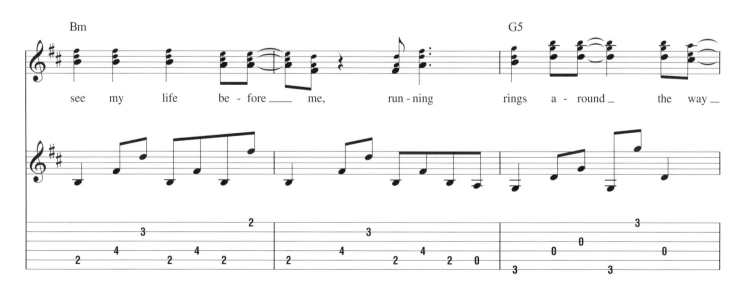

see my life be - fore ___ me, run - ning rings a - round ___ the way ___

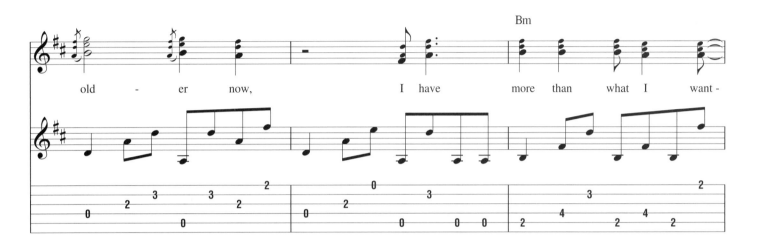

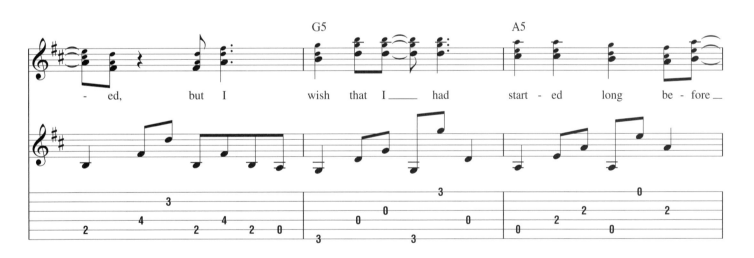

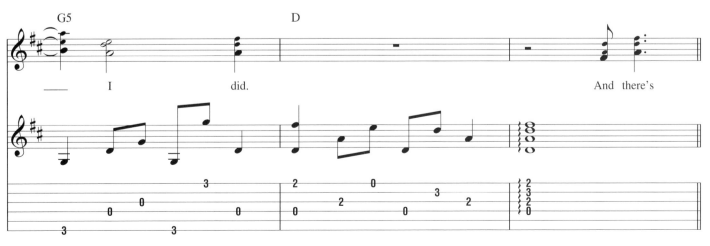

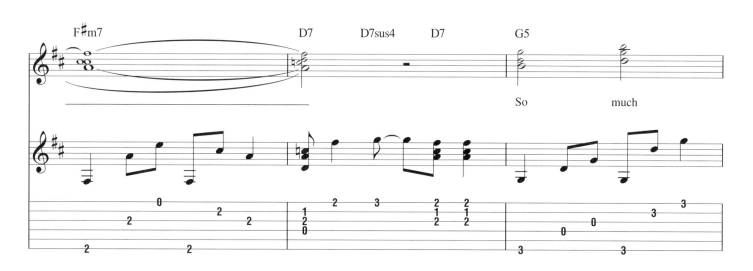

2nd time, substitute Fill 2

wa - ter mov - ing   un - der - neath __ the   bridge. ____

____   Let the wa - ter come __ and   car - ry us __ a - way. __

Violin Solo

To Coda ⊕

w/ pick

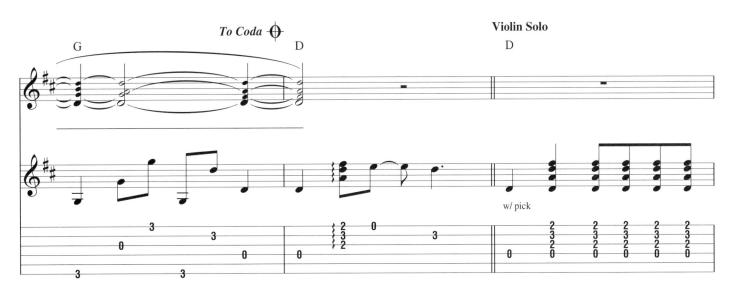

Fill 2

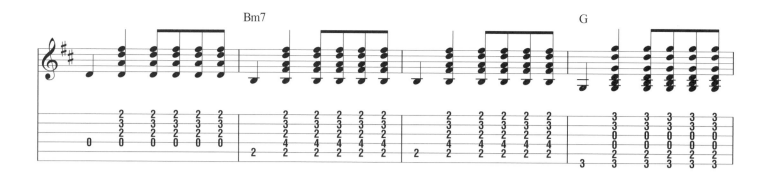

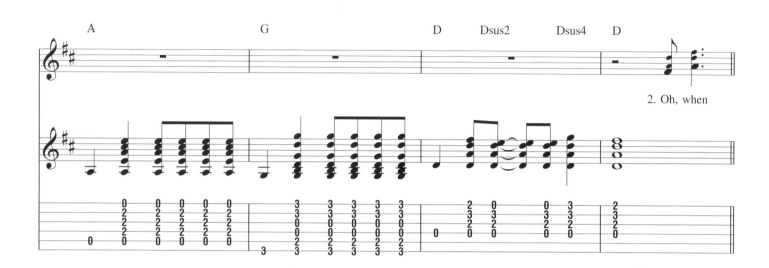

HAL•LEONARD® GUITAR PLAY-ALONG

AUDIO ACCESS INCLUDED

This series will help you play your favorite songs quickly and easily. Just follow the tab and listen to the audio to the hear how the guitar should sound, and then play along using the separate backing tracks. Audio files also include software to slow down the tempo without changing pitch. The melody and lyrics are included in the book so that you can sing or simply follow along.

INCLUDES TAB

VOL. 1 – ROCK	00699570 / $16.99
VOL. 2 – ACOUSTIC	00699569 / $16.99
VOL. 3 – HARD ROCK	00699573 / $17.99
VOL. 4 – POP/ROCK	00699571 / $16.99
VOL. 6 – '90S ROCK	00699572 / $16.99
VOL. 7 – BLUES	00699575 / $17.99
VOL. 8 – ROCK	00699585 / $16.99
VOL. 9 – EASY ACOUSTIC SONGS	00151708 / $16.99
VOL. 10 – ACOUSTIC	00699586 / $16.95
VOL. 11 – EARLY ROCK	00699579 / $14.95
VOL. 12 – POP/ROCK	00699587 / $14.95
VOL. 13 – FOLK ROCK	00699581 / $16.99
VOL. 14 – BLUES ROCK	00699582 / $16.99
VOL. 15 – R&B	00699583 / $16.99
VOL. 16 – JAZZ	00699584 / $15.95
VOL. 17 – COUNTRY	00699588 / $16.99
VOL. 18 – ACOUSTIC ROCK	00699577 / $15.95
VOL. 19 – SOUL	00699578 / $15.99
VOL. 20 – ROCKABILLY	00699580 / $16.99
VOL. 21 – SANTANA	00174525 / $17.99
VOL. 22 – CHRISTMAS	00699600 / $15.99
VOL. 23 – SURF	00699635 / $15.99
VOL. 24 – ERIC CLAPTON	00699649 / $17.99
VOL. 25 – THE BEATLES	00198265 / $17.99
VOL. 26 – ELVIS PRESLEY	00699643 / $16.99
VOL. 27 – DAVID LEE ROTH	00699645 / $16.95
VOL. 28 – GREG KOCH	00699646 / $16.99
VOL. 29 – BOB SEGER	00699647 / $15.99
VOL. 30 – KISS	00699644 / $16.99
VOL. 31 – CHRISTMAS HITS	00699652 / $14.95
VOL. 32 – THE OFFSPRING	00699653 / $14.95
VOL. 33 – ACOUSTIC CLASSICS	00699656 / $17.99
VOL. 34 – CLASSIC ROCK	00699658 / $17.99
VOL. 35 – HAIR METAL	00699660 / $17.99
VOL. 36 – SOUTHERN ROCK	00699661 / $16.95
VOL. 37 – ACOUSTIC UNPLUGGED	00699662 / $22.99
VOL. 38 – BLUES	00699663 / $16.95
VOL. 39 – '80S METAL	00699664 / $16.99
VOL. 40 – INCUBUS	00699668 / $17.95
VOL. 41 – ERIC CLAPTON	00699669 / $17.99
VOL. 42 – COVER BAND HITS	00211597 / $16.99
VOL. 43 – LYNYRD SKYNYRD	00699681 / $17.95
VOL. 44 – JAZZ	00699689 / $16.99
VOL. 45 – TV THEMES	00699718 / $14.95
VOL. 46 – MAINSTREAM ROCK	00699722 / $16.95
VOL. 47 – HENDRIX SMASH HITS	00699723 / $19.99
VOL. 48 – AEROSMITH CLASSICS	00699724 / $17.99
VOL. 49 – STEVIE RAY VAUGHAN	00699725 / $17.99
VOL. 50 – VAN HALEN 1978-1984	00110269 / $17.99
VOL. 51 – ALTERNATIVE '90S	00699727 / $14.99
VOL. 52 – FUNK	00699728 / $15.99
VOL. 53 – DISCO	00699729 / $14.99
VOL. 54 – HEAVY METAL	00699730 / $15.99
VOL. 55 – POP METAL	00699731 / $14.95
VOL. 56 – FOO FIGHTERS	00699749 / $15.99
VOL. 59 – CHET ATKINS	00702347 / $16.99
VOL. 62 – CHRISTMAS CAROLS	00699798 / $12.95
VOL. 63 – CREEDENCE CLEARWATER REVIVAL	00699802 / $16.99
VOL. 64 – THE ULTIMATE OZZY OSBOURNE	00699803 / $17.99
VOL. 66 – THE ROLLING STONES	00699807 / $17.99
VOL. 67 – BLACK SABBATH	00699808 / $16.99

VOL. 68 – PINK FLOYD – DARK SIDE OF THE MOON	00699809 / $16.99
VOL. 69 – ACOUSTIC FAVORITES	00699810 / $16.99
VOL. 70 – OZZY OSBOURNE	00699805 / $16.99
VOL. 73 – BLUESY ROCK	00699829 / $16.99
VOL. 74 – SIMPLE STRUMMING SONGS	00151706 / $19.99
VOL. 75 – TOM PETTY	00699882 / $16.99
VOL. 76 – COUNTRY HITS	00699884 / $14.95
VOL. 77 – BLUEGRASS	00699910 / $15.99
VOL. 78 – NIRVANA	00700132 / $16.99
VOL. 79 – NEIL YOUNG	00700133 / $24.99
VOL. 80 – ACOUSTIC ANTHOLOGY	00700175 / $19.95
VOL. 81 – ROCK ANTHOLOGY	00700176 / $22.99
VOL. 82 – EASY SONGS	00700177 / $14.99
VOL. 83 – THREE CHORD SONGS	00700178 / $16.99
VOL. 84 – STEELY DAN	00700200 / $16.99
VOL. 85 – THE POLICE	00700269 / $16.99
VOL. 86 – BOSTON	00700465 / $16.99
VOL. 87 – ACOUSTIC WOMEN	00700763 / $14.99
VOL. 89 – REGGAE	00700468 / $15.99
VOL. 90 – CLASSICAL POP	00700469 / $14.99
VOL. 91 – BLUES INSTRUMENTALS	00700505 / $15.99
VOL. 92 – EARLY ROCK INSTRUMENTALS	00700506 / $15.99
VOL. 93 – ROCK INSTRUMENTALS	00700507 / $16.99
VOL. 94 – SLOW BLUES	00700508 / $16.99
VOL. 95 – BLUES CLASSICS	00700509 / $15.99
VOL. 96 – BEST COUNTRY HITS	00211615 / $16.99
VOL. 97 – CHRISTMAS CLASSICS	00236542 / $14.99
VOL. 99 – ZZ TOP	00700762 / $16.99
VOL. 100 – B.B. KING	00700466 / $16.99
VOL. 101 – SONGS FOR BEGINNERS	00701917 / $14.99
VOL. 102 – CLASSIC PUNK	00700769 / $14.99
VOL. 103 – SWITCHFOOT	00700773 / $16.99
VOL. 104 – DUANE ALLMAN	00700846 / $16.99
VOL. 105 – LATIN	00700939 / $16.99
VOL. 106 – WEEZER	00700958 / $14.99
VOL. 107 – CREAM	00701069 / $16.99
VOL. 108 – THE WHO	00701053 / $16.99
VOL. 109 – STEVE MILLER	00701054 / $17.99
VOL. 110 – SLIDE GUITAR HITS	00701055 / $16.99
VOL. 111 – JOHN MELLENCAMP	00701056 / $14.99
VOL. 112 – QUEEN	00701052 / $16.99
VOL. 113 – JIM CROCE	00701058 / $16.99
VOL. 114 – BON JOVI	00701060 / $16.99
VOL. 115 – JOHNNY CASH	00701070 / $16.99
VOL. 116 – THE VENTURES	00701124 / $16.99
VOL. 117 – BRAD PAISLEY	00701224 / $16.99
VOL. 118 – ERIC JOHNSON	00701353 / $16.99
VOL. 119 – AC/DC CLASSICS	00701356 / $17.99
VOL. 120 – PROGRESSIVE ROCK	00701457 / $14.99
VOL. 121 – U2	00701508 / $16.99
VOL. 122 – CROSBY, STILLS & NASH	00701610 / $16.99
VOL. 123 – LENNON & McCARTNEY ACOUSTIC	00701614 / $16.99
VOL. 125 – JEFF BECK	00701687 / $16.99
VOL. 126 – BOB MARLEY	00701701 / $16.99
VOL. 127 – 1970S ROCK	00701739 / $16.99
VOL. 128 – 1960S ROCK	00701740 / $14.99
VOL. 129 – MEGADETH	00701741 / $16.99
VOL. 130 – IRON MAIDEN	00701742 / $17.99
VOL. 131 – 1990S ROCK	00701743 / $14.99
VOL. 132 – COUNTRY ROCK	00701757 / $15.99
VOL. 133 – TAYLOR SWIFT	00701894 / $16.99
VOL. 134 – AVENGED SEVENFOLD	00701906 / $16.99

VOL. 135 – MINOR BLUES	00151350 / $17.99
VOL. 136 – GUITAR THEMES	00701922 / $14.99
VOL. 137 – IRISH TUNES	00701966 / $15.99
VOL. 138 – BLUEGRASS CLASSICS	00701967 / $16.99
VOL. 139 – GARY MOORE	00702370 / $16.99
VOL. 140 – MORE STEVIE RAY VAUGHAN	00702396 / $17.99
VOL. 141 – ACOUSTIC HITS	00702401 / $16.99
VOL. 143 – SLASH	00702425 / $19.99
VOL. 144 – DJANGO REINHARDT	00702531 / $16.99
VOL. 145 – DEF LEPPARD	00702532 / $17.99
VOL. 146 – ROBERT JOHNSON	00702533 / $16.99
VOL. 147 – SIMON & GARFUNKEL	14041591 / $16.99
VOL. 148 – BOB DYLAN	14041592 / $16.99
VOL. 149 – AC/DC HITS	14041593 / $17.99
VOL. 150 – ZAKK WYLDE	02501717 / $16.99
VOL. 151 – J.S. BACH	02501730 / $16.99
VOL. 152 – JOE BONAMASSA	02501751 / $19.99
VOL. 153 – RED HOT CHILI PEPPERS	00702990 / $19.99
VOL. 155 – ERIC CLAPTON – FROM THE ALBUM UNPLUGGED	00703085 / $16.99
VOL. 156 – SLAYER	00703770 / $17.99
VOL. 157 – FLEETWOOD MAC	00101382 / $16.99
VOL. 158 – ULTIMATE CHRISTMAS	00101889 / $14.99
VOL. 159 – WES MONTGOMERY	00102593 / $19.99
VOL. 160 – T-BONE WALKER	00102641 / $16.99
VOL. 161 – THE EAGLES – ACOUSTIC	00102659 / $17.99
VOL. 162 – THE EAGLES HITS	00102667 / $17.99
VOL. 163 – PANTERA	00103036 / $17.99
VOL. 164 – VAN HALEN 1986-1995	00110270 / $17.99
VOL. 165 – GREEN DAY	00210343 / $17.99
VOL. 166 – MODERN BLUES	00700764 / $16.99
VOL. 167 – DREAM THEATER	00111938 / $24.99
VOL. 168 – KISS	00113421 / $16.99
VOL. 169 – TAYLOR SWIFT	00115982 / $16.99
VOL. 170 – THREE DAYS GRACE	00117337 / $16.99
VOL. 171 – JAMES BROWN	00117420 / $16.99
VOL. 172 – THE DOOBIE BROTHERS	00119670 / $16.99
VOL. 173 – TRANS-SIBERIAN ORCHESTRA	00119907 / $19.99
VOL. 174 – SCORPIONS	00122119 / $16.99
VOL. 175 – MICHAEL SCHENKER	00122127 / $16.99
VOL. 176 – BLUES BREAKERS WITH JOHN MAYALL & ERIC CLAPTON	00122132 / $19.99
VOL. 177 – ALBERT KING	00123271 / $16.99
VOL. 178 – JASON MRAZ	00124165 / $17.99
VOL. 179 – RAMONES	00127073 / $16.99
VOL. 180 – BRUNO MARS	00129706 / $16.99
VOL. 181 – JACK JOHNSON	00129854 / $16.99
VOL. 182 – SOUNDGARDEN	00138161 / $17.99
VOL. 183 – BUDDY GUY	00138240 / $17.99
VOL. 184 – KENNY WAYNE SHEPHERD	00138258 / $17.99
VOL. 185 – JOE SATRIANI	00139457 / $17.99
VOL. 186 – GRATEFUL DEAD	00139459 / $17.99
VOL. 187 – JOHN DENVER	00140839 / $17.99
VOL. 188 – MÖTLEY CRUE	00141145 / $17.99
VOL. 189 – JOHN MAYER	00144350 / $17.99
VOL. 191 – PINK FLOYD CLASSICS	00146164 / $17.99
VOL. 192 – JUDAS PRIEST	00151352 / $17.99

Prices, contents, and availability subject to change without notice.

Complete song lists available online.

HAL•LEONARD®
www.halleonard.com

0218